she felt like feeling nothing

she felt like feeling nothing

r.h. Sin

scene one.

you're waiting aren't you
you're always waiting for a sign
something that'll help you believe
in him and all of his lies

you're in denial about the truth
never questioning his excuse
say you think highly of yourself
but you still entertain his abuse

what happened to your soul
i see the bruises and the scars
he never deserved to touch your canvas
how'd you forget that you are art

i know it fucking hurts
but i'll just say this because it's true
any man who hurts your heart
is incapable of falling for you

and i know somewhere you agree
this is the hardest lesson learned
thought it was cool to play with fire
but no one warned you that it'd burn

now all the promises were broken
you cut yourself on shards of lies
smiling in every selfie
but inside you scream and cry

now what's a heart to do
when it aches black and blue
you put trust in his hands
but now his hands are harming you

there is love, i hope you find it
it lives within, i hope you find it
that text says, "baby i miss you"
but i hope you know he's lying

think of me a friend
or a stranger who gives a fuck
i just wish to see you grow
i'm tired of seeing you stuck

scene two.

where do you go

when your eyes stare into the moon

where do you go

when your heart feels too heavy

to hold

do you even know how beautiful you are

how the stars envy you

full of a light that shines through darkness

full of life in the dead of night

searching for yourself

lost in a forest of misfortune

and betrayal

you could yell and wake up the sun

and yet you sit silently in the darkness

in deep thought

like a daydream that occurs at night

i wonder where you wander

when you look into the moon

scene three.

she felt like feeling nothing

cold like a touch of winter

empty like the wine bottles

that took up space in her room

a summer of mistakes

led her here

a bed filled with loneliness

and a heart tired of breaking

she felt like feeling nothing

she grew tired missing you

scene four.

just because they're good-looking

doesn't mean they'll be good to you

some things or some bodies

are just nice to look at

but those same things

those same some bodies

could be the same ones

to destroy the joy in your heart

be careful

scene five.

she knows things

she knows so much more

than you realize

noticing it all

and so much of what she sees

has become too much for her heart

she lives with it

your secrets, your lies

the things you've kept hidden

she knows every hiding place

and yet she says nothing

she sits silently

watching you play a losing game

with her heart

one day she'll let you know

what she knows

and that'll be the day

that she's ready to let go

scene six.

i think in some way

the liquor complicated

but somehow complemented

her grief in a temporary way

often drinking whatever she could

with hopes of drowning her demons

and i don't think she was wrong

for searching for a cure

but i do wish she knew

that what she actually needed

was to find more of herself

because at the end of each night

she had always been

the one strong enough

to save her own soul

from the pits of depression

scene seven.

midnight has been harsh

to her heart

betrayed by her own mind

the soul of a woman

damaged by the person

she should have never loved

overthinking herself

into a version of hell

tonight she fights

struggling to survive

but somehow on this night

she'll overcome her troubles

scene eight.

she realized that wanting him

meant losing herself

she realized that she couldn't

save her own soul

because her hands were too busy

holding the hand of someone

who no longer deserved her energy

scene nine.

sometimes you just have to let go

of certain people

in order to make room

for something beautiful

to enter your life

scene ten.

save yourself for yourself

right now

only you deserve you

scene eleven.

i hope you stop caring
when they do
i hope you walk away
because they will

i hope you know
that you'll be fine
and they'll regret
losing a woman like you

scene twelve.

winter calls

the air changes

and the sky turns pale

relationships become complicated

a love turned hell

like seasons changing

love fades like the warmth

of a summer

and now the process begins

the letting go of a lover

scene thirteen.

who were you

before you decided

to let the world

dictate who you'd become

sure enough

you've always been beautiful

and yet you've struggled to see this

because society took your truth

then replaced it with lies

i wish you knew

just how remarkable you are

i wish you knew

just how amazing you already were

before the world

told you who you should be

scene fourteen.

when you go to bed

with strangers

you wake up lonelier

than you previously felt

the heart collapses into itself

filling the void with more emptiness

but the sex, it rarely helps

scene fifteen.

she walked through the fire

wearing nothing but a smile

because she knew damn well

that she'd bring her demons

to their knees

scene sixteen.

deserve me

deserve me

deserve me

scene seventeen.

fight for her

while she still gives a fuck

because one day you'll be too late

scene eighteen.

i think there are times

where you miss the version of yourself

who never knew

what it meant to feel betrayed

scene nineteen.

in you

are poems

that aren't meant

to be read by everyone

scene twenty.

she was more than they could ever comprehend

she was more than she knew

scene twenty-one.

you are more than what you appear to be

you are more than your exterior

there's so much more to you than the surface

scene twenty-two.

you were golden before him

you'll be golden after

scene twenty-three.

i think you outgrew them

your heart finally realized

that being happy

meant letting go

scene twenty-four.

look at you . . .

a heart filled with scars

a soul that's been aching

and yet somehow

you manage to smile

scene twenty-five.

a good heart

with the right love

falling for all

the wrong people

scene twenty-six.

two flowers growing

in opposite directions

a friendship ending

scene twenty-seven.

how easy it is

to become a poet

between the hours

of midnight

and 3 in the morning

scene twenty-eight.

i can feel the weariness

in your fingers

as you turn each page

in this book

searching for something

that'll calm the raging

oceans of negative emotions

living within the temple

of your heart

i feel you

i understand

scene twenty-nine.

she could finally
look to herself
once she realized
that she had everything
she needed

scene thirty.

the moon knows her better
than any man could
she told her secrets
to the night
and kept it all hidden
behind a beautiful smile
during the day

scene thirty-one.

the best revenge

is realizing that you never needed

the person who hurt you

scene thirty-two.

can't argue with silence

it never speaks back

be silent when others

no longer deserve your words

scene thirty-three.

you can't plant yourself
in unhealthy relationships
and expect roses to grow

scene thirty-four.

you're beautiful

even when he doesn't see it

scene thirty-five.

you are not wrong

for wanting someone

who reminds your heart

that it deserves to be loved

scene thirty-six.

my dear

you must learn

to walk away from anyone

who no longer

appreciates your presence

scene thirty-seven.

don't betray yourself
just to protect those
who never protect you

scene thirty-eight.

the sun doesn't feel the same

as it used to

i've been hiding from its light

in search of a shade that'll keep my secrets from
the rest of the world

i used to smile listening to the birds

chirping outside my window

but now their melodies sound like chaos

to my ears

small animalistic reminders

of how happier everything else is

outside of myself and how sad

i've become on a morning where

i should be happy to be alive

but i'm not

my whole life has been about waiting always waiting,
always hanging on

to the tomorrows of today

or trying to figure out how

to survive the aches of yesterday

my past has been riddled with riddles

that i can't solve

and even though

i'm used to this struggle

i'm still fighting to evolve

the rain falls from within

overflowing internally

i'm drowning, slowly consumed

by the sadness of it all

and somehow living in this moment

feels like dying all the same

still mourning.

and you're here

your heart breaking

your weary eyes

staring at the words

on this page

you're in search of something

that'll calm the chaos

that lives within your mind

you're just searching for something

to ease the aches that reside

in your heart

your pain has brought you here

the hurt that dwells in your bones

has brought you here to me

i see you

i hear you

i feel you

i understand

you should be proud of yourself
bending without breaking
falling but finding the strength
to pick yourself up
from a pit filled with broken hearts
and dreams dismantled by the lies
of those incapable
of being honest

your softness is not a weakness
your kindness is your strength
give all of the things
that they've taken for granted
to yourself

because right now
more than anything
you deserve you
it's time to love yourself

echoes of ex.

this isn't what i wanted

i thought i needed you

until i realized

that you never deserved me

after them.

it hurts because you cared

more than you should have

it hurts because your heart

is brave enough to love unconditionally

don't be afraid of the hurt

don't run away from the pain

in the midst of chaos

you'll cultivate peace

after the destruction

you'll rebuild yourself

thank you love.

i know you

you're the girl

with a smile on her face

and sadness in her eyes

you're the girl

refusing to let life

break you

you're the girl

who always survives

you're the one

who inspired these words

and so

i thank God for you

self, July 9th.

she, a rose

she brought herself

to bloom

aperture.

if you want to taste

the universe

just kiss her

July 9th 2017.

and for so long

she had no clue

that all this time

she was always

saving herself

all the mighty.

powerful women are tired

of trying

for lovers who never try

for them

asking the night.

i once spray-painted

your name across the walls

of my heart

all the false sentiments

that appeared to be genuine

still push me to the edge

of insanity

thinking to myself

how could i ever fall

for someone

too weak to catch me

how could i love

someone so empty

for once.

i waited and waited
the moments passed slow
and time slowly faded
like color placed in bleach

second and optional
second and often last
sometimes never picked at all
my pain transformed into anger

i waited and waited
until i couldn't anymore
and there was nothing left
for me to hold on to

you lost me
i lost nothing

my poems are interludes of everything

the heart screams

there is nothing wrong

with the feet

of a woman who would rather

walk toward peace

than run to the middle of chaos

a hymn for her

a melody for the soul

hymn one.

she is deeply daring

a beautiful assortment

of adventures

she's an experience

worth fighting for

hymn two.

one day you'll grow tired

of loving people

who don't love you back

hymn three.

a man who is unsure about

the way he feels for you

is unworthy of a space

in your heart

hymn four.

stop chasing things

that make you lose yourself

hymn five.

he never told her why

but somehow

she always knew

hymn six.

she'd trade in those high heels

for a comfortable pair of socks

and a night of staying in

cuddling on the couch

in the arms of her favorite person

hymn seven.

all of my mistakes were people

who were never what they promised to be

hymn eight.

i couldn't find the words
and so i sat silently
screaming from within
searching for a way out

hymn nine.

you are something
that someone
has been waiting
their entire life for

hymn ten.

her lips didn't have to move

her silence told the story

of a woman who reached

a breaking point

and was no longer willing

to fight for someone

who didn't deserve her effort

hymn eleven.

you can't always see it

but she's fighting something

she's at war within herself

and she refuses to be defeated

hymn twelve.

not all darkness is bad

evil things can travel in the light

hymn thirteen.

it's weird because

whenever we're together

heaven feels real to me

hymn fourteen.

plant kisses on her heart

and watch the flowers grow

hymn fifteen.

decide to be gentle with your own heart

hymn sixteen.

you're just a beautiful misfit

deserving of a love that keeps you free

hymn seventeen.

in a world filled with destruction

you are the perfect distraction

hymn eighteen.

you have to be brave sweetheart

courage looks good on you

hymn nineteen.

you've hidden so much

of what you've felt

in the corners of your heart

refusing to open up

out of fear of being hurt again

hymn twenty.

she held madness like a flower

hymn twenty-one.

we are all mad at something

we've all been betrayed by someone

hymn twenty-two.

she is music

there are melodies inside of her

that most people

don't deserve to hear

hymn twenty-three.

understand that you tried your best

and that will always be enough

even when others are incapable

of appreciating it

hymn twenty-four.

don't be his second option

don't be the one he calls

when no one else answers

hymn twenty-five.

her heart was the only poem

i needed to read

hymn twenty-six.

solitude is a deep romance with self

hymn twenty-seven.

the heart lingers

in the hands of those

incapable of keeping it safe

and i've become one of those people

who falls in love with lies

that sound like the truth

hymn twenty-eight.

some women feel like

a blissful form of chaos

the type of chaos

you want in your life

hymn twenty-nine.

i wish you loved you
as much as you loved him

hymn thirty.

you must awaken your own strength

you have the power to create power

November falls into winter.

beneath the chill in my soul

and the overcrowding of my mind

is a heart that is both afraid

and willing to be loved

i shake like earthquakes

trembling like the weakest spine

i fall like raindrops

or leaves that belong to trees

in November

remember, i am a creature

who has been broken

by the hands of past loves

understand that i am hurting

still trying to recover

still trying to rebuild

standing still, afraid to move forward

and yet i desire to put distance

between myself and what lives behind me

i'm fighting to put distance

between an awful past

and a tough present

as i struggle to look toward

a future in which i'm happy

<u>your sister I.</u>

she's your enemy

and yet she's your sister

bound by blood

altered by jealousy

your sister II.

she's the color green

still managing to see red

while watching you evolve

into everything she'd eventually envy

family is just a word

until those with certain titles

give purpose to those labels

and it just so happens that your sister

would rather play against you

than cheer for you

as you chase after your dreams

could it be that your ability to rise

right before her eyes

has completely twisted her up

with rage growing on the inside

overflowing with the poison of jealousy

noticeably spilling from her

no longer able to keep hidden by fake smiles

and empty compliments

the life after you.

my life ended

the moment i fell for you

and somehow deep down

i realized that in order to live again

i had to live without you

fractured hands.

you're going to hurt yourself

holding on to the same hand

that pushes you closer to heartache

you are here now.

she kept her eyes on the pages

of this book

searching for something to calm

the rage that found its way

into her soul

not knowing that the only thing

worth finding was herself

and this very page

these words were just a reminder

you are her, i know.

what a deadly feeling it must be

to fall heart-first into a space

next to someone incapable

of loving you the way you deserve

and how terrible it must be

to find it difficult

to walk away from someone

you shouldn't stay with

half love, half hurtful.

love doesn't feel like love

when one-sided

love falls short of love

when it isn't reciprocated

and though we may act as if

this half love, this half hurtful

sort of thing is a love

that we can deal with

we later find ourselves feeling empty

and the worst feeling is feeling nothing when all
you want is to feel loved

to love and not be loved in return

is the most destructive kind of love

that type of love is a love

that causes us to lose love for ourselves

believing in him was the mistake

that cost you so much

of your life

too young, so young.

15 or maybe it was 16

possibly younger

your hunger for attention

while being ignored

by those who helped create you

15 or maybe it was 16

possibly younger

the hunger of male counterparts

watching you like prey

reaching for your father's hand

while some young man

destroyed your heart

searching for your mother's voice

but the silence sits in the air

while you claim to love someone

who never truly cared

too young

too hurt

15 or maybe it was 16

these were her memories.

she's starting to remember
she's starting to remember you
in ways she thought she'd forget

she can recall all the pain
caused entirely by you
and your desire
to destroy everything
that was once beautiful
within her

eating away at her appetite
for living
she became a shell of herself
as her skin dried up
and the fat hugging her bones
began to fade

she gave you everything

her entire life force

her soul's energy

invested in a space

that would provide her

with nothing in return

she became a walking skeleton

a dead soul, fighting to live

in the memory of who she was

all because she tried to love you

the raising of self.

a child

a young soul

an innocent heart

forced to raise yourself

in a world content

with misunderstanding you

a child

a young soul

an innocent heart

in need of guidance

and so you reached

for your own hand

because others

have failed you

a voiceless child.

no one hears you

no matter how much you scream

you yell into an empty well

your echoes sound like silence

to those who refuse to listen

you suffocate beneath

the weight of your adolescence

your opinions are weightless

because those opinions

come from the child

and sadly

no one listens

to the kids

3:13:13a.m.

no matter what you do

no matter how hard you try

sometimes no amount of effort

can prevent you from losing

the people you wish to keep

isn't enough.

sometimes being loving

doesn't get you love

and being kind

doesn't bring you kindness

being who you are

being all that you are

will never be enough

for someone

who isn't good enough for you

preferred solitude, alone.

misplaced several times
then discarded like a piece of paper
that ran out of space

it's unfortunate but somehow
you were fortunate to survive
the anguish, the betrayal, the chaos
and the lies

there's still a part of you that resents
the part of yourself that cared
for all the people who never cared
about you

reaching out to them

when they never reached out to you

saying the phone works both ways

but no one reaches out to you

trying, failed

try again, fail some more until you realized that
it was time to only reach for yourself

you became everything

they were incapable of becoming

you are everything

they will never be

and even still, it hurts

the understanding

that being alone

is best and loneliness

is what you now prefer

your family, not family.

they always seem to return

when all the hard work is finished

they add nothing to the journey

but bumps and bruises

and yet they wait for you

at the finish line with their hands open

expecting to be greeted with kindness even when
they've spent most of their energy being unkind
toward you. taking credit for what you've done alone.
taking credit for your joy when all they've ever done

was hurt you

reaching into nothingness.

you're trying

but they rarely make an effort

to match whatever energy

you've invested in the action

of maintaining their interest

you've been fighting

this battle alone

you've been fighting

to keep someone who has yet

to fight for you

these wars

are the most painful of all

these battles

are usually the loneliest

reaching for the same hand

that bruises you

reaching for the same hand

that refuses to reach back

in a sense, you are reaching

into a pit of darkness

a great hole of nothingness

without realizing that the void

in your soul

cannot be filled

with the presence

of an absentminded individual

it began there.

i blame the movies

television shows

and music

for making young girls believe

that bad boys were ideal

and everyone else who failed

to warn them of the blood that they spill

or the things that they take

and the hearts that they break

the compliments

the love and all the things

that they fake

and in the midst of feeling weak

and in the moment of hoping for help

you realized that you alone

have been doing this by yourself

2.3.96.

i'm tired of watching you

force your heart

into unclean hands

expecting an unclean man

to appreciate something so pure

you're too good for him

but you refuse to see it

kept blind by your eagerness

to be everything to a man

who can't do anything for you

but break your heart

and let you down

you're tired but you're too strong

to let go and so you hold on

to something that no longer

deserves to be kept

and i'm just tired

of watching you love someone

who will never love you back

gn.

he texted you right?

claiming to miss you

claiming to care

even though he's rarely there

those lies cause confusion

he chose himself

but you always choose him

a lack of love that kept you hurting

forcing yourself to fix something

that was never working

he texted you right?

only because he's bored

horny, tired of the person

he left you for

claiming to love you

but that's the same man

who left you to fuck someone else

ignore his messages

and he'll text somebody

with the same old lines

the same old lies

that man doesn't deserve your love

sweetheart, open your eyes

5:38:10a.m.

i think you're just

this beautiful misfit

nothing wrong with being different

in search of something real

in search of someone who will listen

someone who will care

someone who will stay

a love that brings you closer

a love that never strays

i think it's beautiful

the way you fight for what you want

the kind of woman who isn't afraid

to request what she deserves

i think you're something rare

out of sorts, far from ordinary

strong-minded, big heart

willing to do the necessary

i know it's been tough

this search for love

will break you down

and i apologize on behalf

of any man who has let you down

22 minutes beyond midnight.

i wish you knew

that in a dark sky

full of stars

you're the only one

worth looking at

i'd sleep all day

if it meant

visiting you in a dream

i know that many men

have attempted the things

i wish to do but i also understand

that most of them

were too weak to fall for you

your eyes like fireflies

simply guiding me

through darkness

like a cart filled with thoughts

searching for a place to park it

i'd like to venture to your garden

plant this seed and watch it grow

i've been searching for someone

like you, a mate for my aching soul

overdosing of heartache.

you were poison

resting in a glass bottle

labeled love

you were the lie

that i believed

but you were never

what i needed

through.

create an exit

and let him leave

he doesn't deserve

to stay

the noise in my head.

it's like waking up
from a good dream
and forcing yourself
back to sleep
in hopes of picking up
where you left off

only to discover
that you can't go back
and no matter
how hard you try
it'll never be the same

the wrong love

makes the poet

want to write

weak and worn.

i think somehow
i've remained there
a place where pain lives
a place where life shouldn't exist
but i've been lost in this
wondering where
wandering here
grieving, once believing in you

confusion crept up in my mind
as i consumed most of your lies
our relationship now tarnished
like weak metals
worn out like old fabric

don't let them play you

like notes

4:54:44p.m.

it happens too much

the doing of so much

for someone

who makes you feel

like your everything

is never enough

i wonder what lies

you told yourself

to keep you in a relationship

that was never meant to last

broken fuse.

aren't you tired

of being this tired

your love taken for granted

your heart continuously aching

all for a love that isn't love

all for someone

who gives you nothing

remembering to forget.

it's hard to forget someone

who used to make your soul smile

but it's even harder to remember

everything they used to be

it rains in her.

it's always raining there
her heart swells with sadness
the joy of this world
escapes her grasp
maybe this is why she holds on
to things that never last
just to feel like she has something
even though that something
is the nothing that makes her feel empty

i think there's a part of me
that aches for her
a part of me that wishes
that i could touch her hand
maybe hold it once
just to remind her
that everything will be fine

you are, you are.

i have something to tell you
one last thing to say here
i have something i need you to know
before i go
before we part
before this ends

you are more than you probably know
you are valuable, just in case you forgot
you are . . . wait hold on . . .

there's a knock at the door . . .

index

#.

2.3.96. 112

3:13:13a.m. 103

4:54:44p.m. 125

5:38:10a.m. 115

22 minutes beyond midnight. 117

a.

after them. 46

all the mighty. 51

aperture. 49

asking the night. 52

a voiceless child. 102

b.

broken fuse. 127

e.

echoes of ex. 45

f.

for once. 53

fractured hands. 92

g.

gn. 113

h.

half love, half hurtful. 95

hymn eight. 64

hymn eighteen. 74

hymn eleven. 67

hymn fifteen. 71

hymn five. 61

hymn four. 60

hymn fourteen. 70

hymn nine. 65

hymn nineteen. 75

hymn one. 57

hymn seven. 63

hymn seventeen. 73

hymn six. 62

hymn sixteen. 72

hymn ten. 66

hymn thirteen. 69

hymn thirty. 86

hymn three. 59

hymn twelve. 68

hymn twenty. 76

hymn twenty-eight. 84

hymn twenty-five. 81

hymn twenty-four. 80

hymn twenty-nine. 85

hymn twenty-one. 77

hymn twenty-seven. 83

hymn twenty-six. 82

hymn twenty-three. 79

hymn twenty-two. 78

hymn two. 58

i.

isn't enough. 104

it began there. 110

it rains in her. 129

j.

July 9th 2017. 50

n.

November falls into winter. 87

o.

overdosing of heartache. 119

p.

preferred solitude, alone. 105

r.

reaching into nothingness. 108
remembering to forget. 128

s.

scene eight. 11
scene eighteen. 21
scene eleven. 14
scene fifteen. 18
scene five. 8
scene four. 7
scene fourteen. 17
scene nine. 12
scene nineteen. 22
scene one. 1
scene seven. 10
scene seventeen. 20
scene six. 9

scene sixteen. 19

scene ten. 13

scene thirteen. 16

scene thirty. 33

scene thirty-eight. 41

scene thirty-five. 38

scene thirty-four. 37

scene thirty-one. 34

scene thirty-seven. 40

scene thirty-six. 39

scene thirty-three. 36

scene thirty-two. 35

scene three. 6

scene twelve. 15

scene twenty. 23

scene twenty-eight. 31

scene twenty-five. 28

scene twenty-four. 27

scene twenty-nine. 32

scene twenty-one. 24

scene twenty-seven. 30

scene twenty-six. 29

scene twenty-three. 26

scene twenty-two. 25

scene two. 4

self, July 9th. 48

still mourning. 43

t.

thank you love. 47

the life after you. 91

the noise in my head. 121

the raising of self. 101

these were her memories. 99

through. 120

too young, so young. 97

w.

weak and worn. 123

y.

you are here now. 93

you are her, i know. 94

you are, you are. 130

your family, not family. 107

your sister I. 89

your sister II. 90

she felt like feeling nothing

copyright © 2018 by r.h. Sin. All rights reserved. Printed in the United States of America. No part of this book may be used or reproduced in any manner whatsoever without written permission except in the case of reprints in the context of reviews.

Andrews McMeel Publishing
a division of Andrews McMeel Universal
1130 Walnut Street, Kansas City, Missouri 64106
www.andrewsmcmeel.com

18 19 20 21 22 RR2 10 9 8 7 6 5 4 3 2

ISBN: 978-1-4494-9425-4

Library of Congress Control Number: 2017963146

Editor: Patty Rice

Art Director: Diane Marsh

Production Editor: David Shaw

Production Manager: Cliff Koehler